la ofrenda
(the offering)

by

josé casas

Dramatic Publishing
Woodstock, Illinois • England • Australia • New Zealand

*** NOTICE ***

la ofrenda (the offering)

ISBN: 1-58342-339-7

this play
is dedicated to
José Cruz González
my mentor
my colleague
and
my friend

IMPORTANT BILLING AND CREDIT REQUIREMENTS

All producers of the Play *must* give credit to the Author of the Play in all programs distributed in connection with performances of the Play and in all instances in which the title of the Play appears for purposes of advertising, publicizing or otherwise exploiting the Play and/or a production. The name of the Author *must* also appear on a separate line, on which no other name appears, immediately following the title, and *must* appear in size of type not less than fifty percent (50%) the size of the title type. Biographical information on the Author, if included in the playbook, may be used in all programs. *In all programs this notice must appear:*

"Produced by special arrangement with
THE DRAMATIC PUBLISHING COMPANY of Woodstock, Illinois"

la ofrenda (the offering)
was a winner of the
2005 IRT Waldo M. and Grace C. Bonderman
Playwriting for Youth National Symposium
and was featured in a rehearsed reading at
the Indiana Repertory Theatre, Indianapolis.

The artistic team that assisted
in the development of this play
included:

Emily Petkewich - Director
Richard Roberts - Dramaturg
Jeff Querin - Assistant Dramaturg
Pat Sanchez - Team Assistant

"Children sweeten labors,
but they make misfortunes more bitter.
They increase the cares of life,
but they mitigate the remembrance of death."

— Frances Bacon

la ofrenda

a play in one act
for 2 men and 1 woman

characters

alex smith: a nine-year old boy. biracial: chicano and white

marta torres: alex's abuelita (grandmother). she is chicana and is in her late fifties. she is a bus driver for the city of los angeles

califas: calavera (skeleton). he is part history, part fantasy. he speaks in calo (urban spanglish). he wears a white oakland raiders football jersey and khaki pants.

time and place

los angeles, california, the fall of 2001.

setting

• the setting consists of two (main) areas. one is the living room of abuelita's house. the other is alex's bedroom which used to be the bedroom of his deceased mother. note: for these two areas, it is recommended that the two bedrooms use as mimimal props as possible. a large papier-mâché calavera/skeleton hangs from the ceiling or against the wall in alex's bedroom. for the living room: a recliner.

- the back of the stage (or back wall) should be used as a projection area. it should be designed as abuelita's backyard. what that means is that the screen should be a clothesline draped with white bed linens, hung at various points with clothes pins, appearing somewhat uneven.

- regardless of where the play is being performed, there should be a trail of marigold petals that leads from the back of the audience to the tip of the stage (performance area).

production notes

note 1: an ofrenda (altar) plays a key role in the play. it should use either a small table or a set of milk crates as its foundation. it should also be covered by a large white decorative sheet of some kind. the items featured on the altar:

- family photos
- candles
- pan dulce/sweetbread
- sugar skulls
- incense
- fruits
- flowers
- tamales
- large figure/statue of la virgen de guadalupe draped by a rosary
- a toy airplane

note 2: there is an acceptance on the playwright's behalf that if this play is performed in an academic institution (K-12), the use of the la virgen de guadalupe icon (as well as the rosary) may become an issue. the playwright agrees to allow the exclusion of these items, but, that being said, the playwright requests that a figure of la virgen de guadalupe still be included on the altar, but out of eyesight in order to preserve and respect the "spirit" of the altar.

also, at one point in the play, the image of the virgen de guadalupe is projected on the clothesline. in cases of public schools presenting, the image of the virgen should be replaced with the image of an eagle silhouette.

any theatre (or institution other than a school) must incorporate the virgen de guadalupe and any other religious items.

note 3: any changes/adjustments to this play must get permission to do so by the playwright and publisher.

la ofrenda (the offering)

scene 1

(sitting in a recliner, located in her living room, is MARTA TORRES. she is a chicana in her late 50's. she is a bus driver for the city of los angeles. her recliner contains side pockets where items such as magazines, remote controls, etc., are contained. she is enjoying the show that is playing on the television.

marta's phone rings. the phone lies in one of the side pockets, but marta is enjoying the show so much that she is ignoring the call. after a few moments, the phone rings again. an annoyed marta grabs the [cordless] phone and checks the caller i.d.; realizing who it is, she ignores the ring again and places the phone back in the pocket. the phone rings a third time. marta figures she will watch the show without any interruptions, but, this time, the ringing doesn't stop so marta finally succumbs to the noise and answers the phone.)

marta. yes, yes, comadre. ya se. it's just that i recorded last weekend's show of sabado gigante and you know much i love don francisco…the tape's been sitting in the vcr since sun— *(it is apparent that the voice on the other line is becoming frantic.)* calmate, comadre! no te aguites. it's too early in the morning. drink your café.

why are you acting so crazy!? *(beat; worried.)* que? what are you talking about? that can't be. what? what channel? todos!? *(marta reaches into the side pocket and clumsily gets the remote control. she is struggling to turn off the vcr so she can watch the breaking news. she finally does so.)* how could this be happening? i don't understand. no entiendo. *(beat.)* lupe, that's where— *(marta drops the phone; extended beat. in shock; to herself.)* jason. *(beat.)* estrella…

(the room goes dark with the only light being that of the television screen. as marta stares at the television screen, the sounds of news reports [of the 9/11 tragedy] can be heard. after a few moments, the stage fades to black as the sounds linger and, eventually, fade.)

scene 2

(the sounds of rustling keys can be heard. after a few moments, we hear a door open, then close. marta enters and then crosses the living room and throws her keys on the magazine stand.)

marta. well…what do you think?
alex. …
marta *(turning toward the door)*. alex?

(beat. a young boy, ALEX SMITH, enters. he is holding a new york yankees lunchbox. alex looks stoically around the room. there is a noticeable tension in the air; beat.)

marta. it's all right, mijo…we're here. *(marta exits and returns with two suitcases. she places them on the floor.)* i know it's not much, but it suits me just fine. are you thirsty, mijo? i can get you some pepsi or maybe a little bit of water?

alex. …

marta. you know, sooner or later you're going to have to say something.

alex. …

marta *(annoyed)*. que vamos hacer con este muchachito? *(beat.)* we need some light.

(marta opens up the blinds as light filters throughout. as she does the light from outside immediately "hits" alex's eyes. he responds by covering his eyes; dropping his lunchbox. marta crosses to pick up the lunchbox, but alex quickly gets in her way and blocks her; extended beat. alex picks up his lunchbox and begins looking around the house.)

marta. i see…well, why don't we put away our things? *(marta grabs her suitcase and exits to her bedroom. from offstage:)* this will have to do for right now, mijo. the rest of your things will get here by next week. *(beat.)* you'll see…everything will turn out for the best. leave your bag in your room and i'll help you unpack later.

(marta returns. alex remains standing in the middle of the living room. he has no "real" recollections of the place. marta can sense this and is a bit saddened by the fact; beat.)

marta. si, como no…it's been so long, mijo. how could you remember. *(marta picks up alex's suitcase and takes it to the door of alex's bedroom. she places it on the floor.)* this room is yours. es para usted y para nadien mas. tu eres el rey de este espacio. entiendes?

alex. … *(extended beat.)*

marta. haven't you been keeping up with your spanish?

alex. …

marta. but…your mama said she was teach— *(awkward beat.)* well, mister. let's make sure that doesn't continue. we can't let that happen…not in los angeles. that's for sure. there are too many people in this city and they all speak a different language, mijo. you need to discover how to talk to the gente. *(proudly.)* look at me. i do it all the time when i'm driving my bus… i know bits and pieces of, at least, ten languages: english, spanish, chinese, korean y chicano; que lo que sea. I'm going to teach you…okay?

alex. …

marta. como no, then…that's the plan, stan. *(alex looks away toward the window that looks over the backyard. marta notices and crosses to the window. encouraged:)* it's the backyard, alex. *(alex hesitantly crosses to the window.)* alejandro… it's not so bad, you'll see. *(beat.)* this is your backyard, mijo…your own space.

alex *(quiet desperation)*. I miss home. *(extended beat. alex touches the window.)* when can I go back home?

scene 3

(alex is sitting on his bed, his lunchbox is open. he is looking over some baseball cards. his abuelita knocks on the door. he quickly closes his lunchbox.)

marta. it's abuelita, can I come in?
alex. i guess.
marta. it's such a beautiful day, alejandro. why don't you go out a—
alex *(annoyed)*. my name is alex. I told you a million times already.
marta. i'm sorry, alex…you're right. you did tell me. *(beat.)* would you like some menudo? or some hand-made tortillas? why don't I make you a special treat?
alex. i don't eat mexican food.
marta. then…how about a peanut butter and jelly sandwich?
alex. no…mom is the only one who makes my sandwiches. she does it a special way.
marta. okay, then i won't ask until you do…you're the boss, mijo. *(beat.)* i like your lunchbox. where did you get it?
alex. …
marta. did your mama get it for you?
alex. i got it with dad…at the ball game.
marta *(beat)*. pues, like i said before, it's a beautiful day to-day. why don't we go out back and throw the baseball around? i know you like baseball.
alex. you're a girl.
marta. and…you're a boy. what's your point?
alex. …
marta. who do you think taught your mama to throw?

alex. yeah, right.

marta. de veras. she played with the boys until she was thirteen. she made all-stars every year. she was that good.

alex. no, she didn't!

marta. she loved baseball…and, she loved the dodgers. *(beat; excited.)* that's it! why don't you and i go to a dodgers game? there's still a few more games lef—

alex *(offended)*. the dodgers suck!

marta. alejandro! we don't use that type of language…not in this house!

alex. sorry. *(beat.)* the yankees are my team.

(extended beat; marta begins looking around the room.)

marta. i'm impressed, mijo. every time i come in your room it's always so neat.

alex *(annoyed)*. it's not my room.

marta. well, then, mr. smart mouth. who's is it then?

alex. it's mom's room…right?

marta *(quietly)*. it was…once.

alex. that's what i said.

marta *(playing along)*. i suppose you're right.

alex. i know i am.

marta. it belongs to your mama…until you decide that you want it.

alex. what?

marta. look around. the room's the same color it's always been—pink! *(beat.)* i can't imagine a proud muchacho like you would enjoy sleeping in a pink girl's room.

alex. i don't care.

marta. estrella's dolls are still on the dresser. *(beat.)* you know, i'm glad you don't want this room. these dolls make me happy. they should stay.

alex. whatever.

marta *(pointing to the calavera)*. well, then, i guess i'll just leave you and your friend alone.

alex. what? that thing?

marta. that thing is not a thing…that is califas.

alex. who?

marta. califas the calaca…the skeleton.

alex. i don't care what his name is.

marta. your mama built him in the fifth grade.

alex. i don't like it.

marta. she did it all by herself. califas was her best friend.

alex. that's lame!

marta *(to califas)*. that's all right, califas. he doesn't understand, but don't worry. no te preocupes…you are staying put.

alex. no way!

marta. si, como no que no way…i don't think so.

alex. but, he gives me the creeps, grandma.

marta. you called me gra…

alex. what?

marta *(beat; pleased)*. oh, nothing, mijo.

alex. so…you'll get rid of this thing.

marta. sorry, buddy. since this isn't your room. you have no say. you said so yourself.

alex. that's not fair!

marta. neither is life, mijo…lesson number one. *(beat.)* i believe i will let you borrow this room…for the time being. *(marta exits the bedroom.)*

scene 4

(alex is lying on his bed staring at the ceiling. marta is running around the other areas of the house in a mad dash—trying to get ready for work, preparing alex's lunch and searching for her keys; all at the same time. she is dressed in her work uniform.)

marta *(yelling)*. alex! hurry up, mijo. i'm going to be late for work. *(looking at her watch.)* chihuahua! i'm already ten minutes late. alex! do you hear what i'm saying!?

alex. …

marta. don't make me go in there!

alex *(annoyed)*. i'm coming!

marta. what do you want for lunch? ham sandwich. a burrito? que quieres!?

alex. nothing!

marta. you didn't want breakfast, so you have to eat lunch. it's important to be healthy, mijo!

alex. i'm not hungry!

marta. aye, muchacho! you're going to be the death of me! *(marta's search for her keys becomes more desperate and she begins to look in every available space possible; to herself:)* my keys! i can't believe this. cada mañana. every morning. it never fails. *(making the sign of the cross.)* what i need is my own personal saint anthony, patron saint of lost keys and, in my case, lost causes. aagh! *(beat.)* alex, come on! the school doesn't run on chicano time!

alex. what's chicano time!?

marta. aye, que la— *(marta finally finds her keys: the keys which are on a chain that connect to marta's belt loop.*

annoyed; to herself.) no me digas! *(beat; yelling.)* alex! let's go!

(alex meanders into the living room. he is carrying his lunchbox.)

marta. i thought you said you weren't hungry.
alex. i'm not.
marta. then…porque con el lunchbox?
alex. i don't use it for lunch. i just use it. *(beat.)* for stuff.
marta. i don't have time to argue with you now. here. *(marta pulls out some money and then shoves it into alex's pocket.)*
alex. what's that for?
marta. for lunch.
alex. i said i wasn't hungry.
marta. just in case…okay. let's go.

(marta walks out of the living room. alex's mood has changed from annoying to nervous. he just stands there in silence like a deer in headlights; extended beat. marta reenters.)

marta. what's the problem?
alex. please don't make me go.
marta. alex…you have to go. it's your first day in the new school and you're already behind as it is. if you miss any more, they'll make you repeat the fourth grade.
alex. but…i don't know anybody.
marta. june from next door is in your class. you said, "hi" to her a few days ago.
alex. it's not my school.

marta. it is now.

alex. no…i don't feel so good. i think i got a fever.

marta. alex…no more games. andale! *(marta grabs alex by the arm. alex doesn't budge.)*

alex *(yelling)*. don't make me go! i don't want to go!

marta. alex, grandma's boss isn't going to be happy! do you want me to get fired!?

alex. i don't care!

marta. no more joking around!

alex. please, grandma!

marta. alex! you're going to school whether you like it or not!

alex. you can't tell me what to do! your not my moth—

(marta slaps alex across the face; the regret instantly sets in; awkward and extended beat. alex, face red, stares silently at his grandmother.)

marta *(tearing up)*. mijo, i'm sorry! i didn't mean…please, tell me you forgive me?

alex. … *(extended beat.)*

marta. mijo…things are different. they are never going to be the same…sabes? your parents are not coming back. *(beat; solemnly.)* this is not a vacation.

alex. …

marta. we are the only ones left, mijo. entiendes que te digo? it's just me and you.

alex *(takes a couple of steps back from marta, coldly)*. i hate you.

(before marta can finish her sentence, alex storms out of the living room to the outside world, leaving a dis-

traught marta, alone with her thoughts; extended beat. marta exits.)

scene 5

(marta is talking on the phone with her comadre. she is upset. sympathy cards litter the floor. alex is lying on his bed and throwing a baseball up into the air.)

marta. what can i do? que hago, lupe?

(alex throws the baseball up, but it drops and rolls onto the floor near the door of his room which is slightly opened. alex picks up the ball and hears that marta is talking on the phone. he quietly stands by the door and begins to eavesdrop on the conversation.)

marta. what was estrella thinking? alejandro no sabe espanol…not one single word. lo puedes creer? a grandson of mine not knowing his own language? a daughter of mine not teaching him? it's a sin…and, that husband of hers. he wasn't even chicano. *(beat.)* honestly, lupita. i can't believe you said that. *(angrily.)* no! you don't understand. i am not overreacting! out of all the nice mexican boys in the barrio she could've chosen, she had to go out and find him…ese huerito. *(beat.)* do you remember josé lopez? yes! juanita's son. si, the doctor. did you know that he was madly in love with estrella? the pobrecito would come to me, almost in tears. that's how much he loved her, but estrella only had eyes for him as a friend. such a respectful and intelligent boy and he turned into such a good-looking man, as well. how could estrella not marry that boy!? *(resentful.)* jason was the one who took them away from me, lupe, and now look… my nieto wants nothing to do with me. his own abuelita. his flesh and blood. *(beat; fondly.)* i can still remember holding alejandro in my arms on the day he was born, he was so small and beautiful and brown…my little angelito. *(beat.)* i don't know what to think anymore. *(marta begins to tear up. she takes out a tissue and dabs her eyes; extended beat.)* it feels like I'm living with a stranger.

(alex is "stung" by these last few words. he dejectedly crosses back to bed and sits down. he opens up his lunchbox and pulls out a picture of his parents; staring at it.)

scene 6

(it's late at night. the sounds of a rainstorm can be heard. alex is in his bed, but he is nowhere close to falling asleep. the audience can see the rain visualized on the clothesline. the silhouette of a tree swaying can also be seen. it is obvious that alex is a little scared so he begins to stare at the ceiling; talking to himself in an attempt to fall asleep.)

alex. old old yankee. willie randolph. second baseman. was on yankee championship teams of seventy-seven and seventy-eight. mariano rivera. greatest yankee reliever of all time…should have a cy young award, but doesn't.

(thunder is heard. alex covers up a little more.) derek jeter. shortstop. drafted by the yankees in the first round. scored a hundred and four runs in his rookie season… dated mariah carey like for a few weeks.

(louder thunder can be heard. all the lights on the street go out, leaving the bedroom pitch black; beat. the lightning begins. the light from the storm is reflecting on califas, causing a "spooky" type of atmosphere. alex wants to call out for his grandmother, but doesn't. the lightning and thunder get worse and alex becomes more scared as it does. he notices califas shaking during one of the bursts of lightning. after a few moments, alex gets out of bed. he slowly walks toward the papier-mâché figure. he gets within inches of califas; beat. he touches califas, then jumps back a few steps; beat. he walks up to califas and touches him again.)

alex. you're not so bad. you don't scare me. *(another round of thunder. alex jumps; begins looking around the room as if he is checking for something. he walks back to califas, then pushes him.)* you ain't so tough.

(thunder. CALIFAS comes to life.)

califas. hey, vato…what's your problem!?
alex *(screaming at the top of his lungs)*. grandma!!!

(alex runs away from califas and goes to the door but is having problems opening it so he runs back into bed and pulls the cover over his head. for a few moments, there

is nothing, but silence, then the tapping of a tree against the window is projected. marta enters disheveled.)

marta. alex. que pasa? what's the matter!?
alex. ...marta digame...tell me.
alex *(pointing to califas)*. that thing...it's alive.
marta. what in god's sake are you talking about?
alex. mom's skeleton...it's alive.
marta. alex, mijo, this isn't funny. it's late and I'm tired.
alex. I'm not lying. it's true. he talked to me.

(marta crosses toward califas and for the sake of alex, touches califas to prove to him that califas is not real. she looks at alex, shaking her head.)

alex. but, grandma...i saw it with my own two eyes!
marta *(unconvinced)*. if you say so. *(the wind gets a little louder and the tree branch begins hitting the window again. marta crosses to the window.)* aye, alex...look! it was the branch hitting the window, mijo. it's nothing to worry about. this big old tree scared your mama tambien when there was a storm...you were just imagining things.
alex. no, i wasn't, grandma.
marta *(sits next to alex on the bed)*. it's all right. i know how storms can be scary. it happens to all of us. it still happens to me once in a while.
alex. i know what i saw.
marta. in fact, i'm a little scared right now. how about you keep your abuela company and bunk up in my room tonight?
alex. no way...i'm not a little kid.

marta. all right, then. *(marta gets up and crosses to the dresser and pulls out a small flashlight. she goes and gives it to alex.)* like i said…your mama went through the same thing, but i'm leaving the door open all the same.

alex *(annoyed)*. i'm not scared.

marta. you're very brave, mijo. *(beat.)* but…you know where i am if you need me. *(beat. alex nods his head.)* que dios de bendiga, mijo.

(marta exits. the sound of the rain is still present. the scene ends with a vigilant alex pointing the flashlight directly at the inanimate califas.)

scene 7

(spotlight on an answering machine. VOICES can be heard.)

marta's voice *(os)*. hola…you've reached the torres household. marta and alex are not in at the moment. por favor deja su mensaje y numero…please leave a message and a number where we can reach you. have a nice day. *(perky.)* adios!

(a series of messages can be heard.)

message 1 *(os)*. aye, comadre…the compadre and i just got back from zacatecas. doña elena told us what happened to estrella and her esposo. we are so sorry…if there is anything we can— *(message erased.)*

message 2 *(os)*. hello…my name is thomas and i am a representative of rockford communications with a great offer for your entire family. for only thirty dollars a month you can g— *(message erased.)*

message 3 *(os)*. is johnny in? johnny? can you hear me? johnny? who's the old broad on the answering machine? johnny, is this even your numb— *(message erased.)*

message 4 *(os)*. hello…miss torres. this is matthew debarry from the offices of randle, miller and duncan. this message is in regards to the estate of jason smith and estrella torres-smith. we've made numerous calls to your residence but have not been successful in reaching you. please, miss torres, i know that this must be a difficult time for you, but these matters have to be addressed in a timely fashion. you can fax over the documents i fed-exed you last week or you can call our office if you have any questions. our number again is 212— *(the machine stops. the play button is pressed.)*

answering machine voice *(os)*. you have one saved message.

scene 8

(in the darkness, the smell of incense fills the stage. a mexican corrido can be heard in the background. lights go up. there is an altar in honor of dia de le muertos/ day of the dead in the living room. it's partially built. marta places a picture on the altar, alex enters as the music fades away.)

marta. how was school, mijo?

alex. …
marta. okay, i won't ask. *(beat.)* what do you think?
alex. about what?
marta. about our ofrenda…our altar.
alex. it smells.
marta. that is the sage and copal, mijo. it helps purify our space.
alex. it still smells.
marta. haven't you ever seen an altar before?
alex. nope.
marta. your mama never told you the stories of our altares? never built one?
alex. no.

(extended beat. marta places another item on the altar.)

marta. how was school today?
alex. you just asked me that?
marta. yes, yes…of course, i forgot… i'm sure you have a lot of homework to take care of. if you need anything, well, ya sabes, you know the deal.

(marta turns her back to alex and begins working on the altar again. alex begins walking to his room and turns around curiously; beat.)

alex. i don't get what the big deal is?
marta. the yearly offering to the ancestors is very important, mijo.
alex. you do this every year?
marta. si dios quiere. *(beat.)* so…are you interested in helping your abuela?

alex. i didn't say that.

marta. your mama used to help me all the time. she was a great helper. i think you would be, too.

alex. i'd mess it up.

marta. nonsense.

alex. plus…it's just a bunch of junk anyways.

marta. junk? junk means trash and this is not trash. *(annoyed.)* entiendes, muchachito.

alex. all right. what's this stuff? whatever.

marta. it's not whatever…these are the treasures we offer up in prayer.

alex. like in church?

marta. almost, but not quite.

alex. what's the point?

marta. it's for dia de los muertos…the day of the dead. *(marta grabs a sugar skull and places it on the altar.)*

alex. you do all this for halloween?

marta. no, alex…halloween has nothing to do with this day and has nothing to do with this altar…this is different. *(beat.)* this is a part of who we are. get my drift? *(alex shrugs his shoulders.)* entonces…enough talking. it's time for you to help me with the altar.

alex. do i have to?

marta. no, but what would you rather be doing right now, helping me with this or doing your time tables?

alex. good point.

marta *(pointing)*. can you go over to the counter and get me that bowl of fruit, mijo? *(alex crosses and retrieves the bowl. he gives it to marta who begins strategically placing each piece of fruit on the altar. after a moment, she gives alex a pear.)* here…find the perfect spot for this.

alex. why are you asking me? i don't know where to put it.
marta. don't think about it…just feel where it should go.
alex. but…it's just a pear.
marta. to you, maybe…to me, this little piece of fruta is a picture i see every time i close my eyes. *(beat; fondly.)* i place pears on the ofrenda in honor of your grandfather. it was his favorite fruit. when we were first courting—
alex. courting? you like basketball.
marta. courting is dating, mijo.
alex *(embarrassed)*. oh.
marta. your grandfather was so poor that he picked pears from his neighbor's casa and gave them to me as a gift because he couldn't afford flowers. aye, your abuelito. he may not have had a lot of money, but he sure was a charmer. *(beat.)* you do you remember your abuelito, don't you?
alex. no.
marta. not even a little?
alex. i don't remember.
marta. como no, mijo…you were just a baby. i forgot.
alex *(hands the pear to marta)*. i think, maybe…you should be the one who puts this on.

(marta nods and then meticulously finds a space for the pear.)

marta. alex…this is a time for remembering, this is why we are here. this altar…it is a remembering space.
alex. why remember?
marta. so…that we never forget.
alex *(beat)*. forgetting isn't such a bad thing.

(marta crosses to alex and tries to hug him, but he steps away in refusal; extended beat.)

marta. you must never think that, mijo.
alex. i don't want to re— *(beat.)* never mind.
marta. it's okay to talk, alex.
alex. that's all anyone ever wants to do nowadays…talk.
marta. talking is what connects us.
alex. no it doesn't.
marta. that's not true, mijo.
alex. yes, it is. people talk all the time. i see it on the news. but, people talk so much they start to fight. when they start to fight, they hurt each other…and, then things change forever.
marta. it's not that simple, mijo. it's more complicated than that.
alex. i'm tired of talking. I'm tired of people thinking i'm weird because i don't want to talk. I'm tired of people i don't know asking me questions…why can't they just leave me alone!?
marta. alex.
alex. why do you let them do that to me, grandma? i thought you liked me.
marta. mijo…i love you.
alex *(quietly pleading)*. then…make them stop talking to me.
marta. i can't, mijo…it's for your own good. they need to talk to you.
alex. no more talking.
marta. they're trying to help you.
alex. they make everything…worse. *(beat; dejectedly.)* are we done with this thing yet?

(extended beat. marta picks up a small transistor radio. she hands it to alex.)

marta. this is the last thing for the day. it belonged to your mama…she would sneak this into her room after her bedtime when she wanted to listen to the dodgers play on the radio.

alex *(fidgets with the transistor radio. angrily)*. this doesn't belong on your stupid altar!

(alex runs into his bedroom with the transistor radio. a worried marta makes no attempt to talk to him. she begins to sob quietly.)

scene 9

(alex is sitting at his school desk and is aggressively coloring a picture. marta is in her living room dusting. she picks up a picture of her late husband: carlos.)

marta. aye, viejo…i wish you were here. necesito to ayuda. I'm scared for our little alejandro. the school counselor says alex should be in therapy. he needs to figure out about all the things running around in his head. i feel so helpless. i don't know what to do or what to say. I'm just a bus driver. nada mas. I'm too old. i have a thousand dollars in the bank. es todo…how will i manage? *(extended beat.)* aye, querido…alex drew this picture in school. it was as if he was drawing a nightmare. a child should never have to experience such cosas in a lifetime. when his teacher showed me the drawing, i wanted to cry, but i couldn't…not in front of him. i need to be strong. i need to protect my little angel. he's the only thing i have left of estrella. he's the only thing i have in this world. *(beat.)* how can i be both mama and papa to him? viejo, if you were around maybe things would be different. a boy needs a man in his life, sabes? *(beat.)* mi amor, please send me the strength i need to raise our grandson.

(marta kisses the photo and places it back in its place. she exits; beat. alex finishes coloring his picture. projected on the clothesline is a drawing: two large buildings exploding with clouds surrounding the top portions of the building. the drawing also includes birds flying away, stick people figures running away from the buildings and, finally, the letters c.n.n. on the bottom. alex stares at the drawing for a bit, then crumples it up in a ball; throwing it to the ground. he dejectedly lays his head on the desk. lights fade to black.)

scene 10

(the stage is dark. war's "slippin into darkness" begins playing. lights up, but the room is still dimly lit. alex is sleeping. califas is dancing his slow "homeboy"-style dance; grooving to the music. little by little, the music gets louder to the point that it wakes up alex. a startled alex stands up in his bed.)

alex *(scared)*. grandma said you weren't real!

(califas ignores him; continues to dance. alex tries to yell out to his grandmother, but for some reason, the words won't come out. alex jumps off his bed and grabs a wiffle-ball bat and begins swinging madly even though he is across the room. califas finally notices alex and is amused by his horrible batting style; beat. califas snaps his fingers and the music abruptly ends.)

califas. hey, little vato…don't playa hate the old school. simon…like take a chill pill…for real.

(alex ignores califas and charges after him. alex begins swinging at califas with the wiffle-ball bat, but califas holds him away at arm's length. califas feigns being hurt.)

califas. ouch…ooch…please, ese, stop…you're killin me. *(alex continues swinging. after a few moments, a bored califas steps to the side and alex falls to the floor.)*

califas *(looking down)*. really, little vato…violence is no way to solve your problems.

alex. leave me alone!

califas. i can…but, i won't.

alex. please, mister.

califas. mister…i like the way that rolls off the tongue. it makes me sound respectable.

alex *(standing up)*. i'm gonna get my grandma.

califas. knock yourself out…she likes me better anyway.

alex. this has to be a nightmare. *(closing his eyes; to himself.)* wake up. wake up. wake up!

califas. that ain't gonna help.

alex. who are you?

califas. boy, you better recognize! *(beat.)* what's my name again?
alex *(beat; cautiously)*. califas.
califas. yeah...that's what i thought.
alex. what do you want with me?
califas. you bein in this room. you're crampin up my estilo...my style, homeboy.
alex. this is my room.
califas. it's not.
alex. it is.
califas. it's not.
alex. it is!
califas. it's estrella's room!

(extended beat. alex walks over to the window and stares out into the sky.)

alex *(sadly)*. estrella.
califas. estrella.
alex. she's my mom.
califas. she...was your mom, ese.
alex *(angrily)*. stop it!
califas. your dad, too.
alex. shut up!
califas. don't bite my head off, carnalito...i'm just the messenger.
alex. they're coming back... i know they are.
califas. this ain't no book, carnalito...you can't rewrite the ending.
alex. they could still be ali—
califas. they aren't.
alex. how can you be so sure?

califas. trust me on this one, little homey.

alex. maybe, someone will see her flier. maybe, they'll recognize their picture. *(beat; defeated.)* maybe...they'll call me.

califas. they won't.

alex. you're lying!

califas. you can't live the rest of your life hopin for something that ain't never gonna happen, carnalito.

alex. i want my mom and dad here with me.

califas. sorry, vato. those are the breaks. como se dice...es la vida.

alex. they can't be gone, i won't let them.

califas. all you're left with are the memories, carnal.

alex. don't say that.

califas. don't trip out, carnalito. it ain't such a bad thing... that's the beauty of memories. no one can take them away from us. not even the tax man...nobody.

alex. it hurts so much.

califas. chale, no one said the system was perfect. *(extended beat.)*

alex *(quietly)*. so...you knew my mom?

califas. simon...the girl was all that and a bag of chips.

alex. can you tell me something about her? something i don't know.

califas. you shouldn't hear it from my lips.

alex. why?

califas. i'm not the family photo album, ese. i got responsibilities, sabes? i'm a popular vato this side of town.

alex. i want to know.

califas. you got a whole lifetime to find out, carnalito...besides, what you are askin is not my job...that chore, little man, belongs to your abuelita.

alex. who says?
califas. this ain't burger king, carnalito…you can't have it your way.
alex. i don't want to. *(beat; sadly.)* talk to her.
califas. that ain't an option.
alex. who says?
califas. destiny says so, ese…you know, blood is thicker than water and all that jive.
alex. you can't make me believe that!
califas. don't worry, little alejandro. i wasn't going to try. *(beat; annoyed.)* shoot…do i look like a babysitter to you?
alex. …
califas. you need to keep your eyes on the road ahead of you, homey.
alex. what road?
califas. the one you must walk…it's the path from birth to death and all that lies in between.
alex. i don't get it.
califas. no one…ever really truly gets it, vato…that's the problem. we all gotta have a little faith and wing it. if you want to wing it alone, well, that's on your shoulders.
alex. i don't know her.
califas. really, carnalito…this is your abuelita we're talking about. i don't know why you're turnin this into a mexican novela.
alex. where was she when i was growing up, huh?
califas. it doesn't work that way, carnalito…things aren't always what they seem.
alex. if my grandma really loved us she would've moved closer to us.

califas. and…leave her home? the only home she's known her entire life?

alex. yeah.

califas. you make it sound so easy, carnalito.

alex. it is.

califas. did you want to leave the only home you've known your entire life?

alex *(beat; hurt)*. no.

califas. see, little alex. that's the point. everybody has reasons for doin the things they do. whether or not you know what those reasons are don't matter…you just gotta learn to respect those decisions.

alex. what do i do now?

califas. only you can answer that, carnal.

alex. but…i have so many questions.

califas. don't we all? *(checking an imaginary watch.)* orale pues, vato…i gotta go. my girl's waitin for me.

alex. please, don't go.

califas *(begins to exit)*. stay…go…chale, ese, you gotta make up your mind.

alex. my mom! *(beat; quietly.)* my parents.

califas *(stops; facing away from alex)*. now is not the time, homey.

alex *(unconvincing)*. we're going to be a family again.

califas. is that what you think?

alex. i hope so.

califas. hopin doesn't pay the bills, alejandro.

alex. califas?

califas. yeah?

alex. just one thing. *(beat.)* tell me one thing about my mom…anything.

califas *(turns around toward alex)*. just one thing? *(alex nods his head.)* i probably shouldn't be sayin this…pero, i do remember this one thing your mom used to do. she was about the same age you are right now.

alex. what? what was it?

califas *(pointing)*. look at the wall. what do you see?

alex. it's just a bunch of scribbling.

califas. i think not, ese…take a closer look.

alex *(steps toward the wall, struggling to read what is on it)*. who is fer…ferna…fernando…valen…valentine?

califas. fernando valenzuela, fool!

alex. sorry…jeez. *(beat.)* who is he?

califas. chale, little man. you're goin to be the life of me! who is fernando valenzuela!? he's only the greatest pitcher in dodgers history.

alex. okay…so what?

califas. so…look at what's written underneath that.

(a baseball box score is projected on the clothesline. it reads as follows:)

4/27/81
SF 1 3 1
LA 5 9 0

alex. whoa…mom wrote down the box score. the dodgers beat the giants five to one.

califas. your grandparents loved takin your mom to the ballgame…just like your parents liked takin you, que no?

alex *(sadly)*. yeah. *(beat.)* we went to a lot of them.

califas. sounds nice.

alex. i remember this one time. *(beat.)* against our biggest enemies…the boston red sox.

califas. was estrella there?

alex. yep. *(extended beat.)*

califas. something wrong?

alex. my dad caught a foul ball in his glove and he handed it to me. *(beat; fondly.)* then…he kissed my mom in front of the whole stadium…they got their pictures shown on the video scoreboard.

califas. sounds nice…did the bronx bombers win?

alex. i don't remember. *(beat.)* that was the last game we ever went to…we were supposed to go to the final home stand of the season against the orioles, but…

califas. i know, carnalito.

alex. the game was cancelled.

califas. even life gets rained out, alejandro.

alex *(barely audible)*. i guess.

(califas pulls out a pen and crosses to alex; handing it to him. califas walks to the window. he stops.)

califas *(tenderly)*. remember, homey…don't let the one game that wasn't…erase all those games…that were. *(beat.)* it's not worth the effort.

(califas quietly exits; extended beat. alex walks to the wall and begins writing a box score on the wall which is projected on the clothesline. it reads as follows:

PPD RAIN
9/10/01
BAL 0 0 0
NY 0 0 0

lights fade to black except for a spotlight on the box score; beat. the light on the box score slowly fades away.)

scene 11

(alex opens the door to the living room. he's just gotten out of school. he places his lunchbox and backpack on the floor, he looks around the room.)

alex *(calling out)*. hello? is anybody home? grandma!?

(alex begins searching the rest of the house. there is still no sign of his grandmother; beat. alex begins to look around at the ofrenda; truly looking at it for the first time. he looks at the pictures and candles. he begins circling the altar for a better glimpse. as he does, califas enters, but he follows behind alex; making sure not to be seen. after a moment, califas grabs a stash of tamales that are on top of the altar. califas, makes a gesture and a silhouette of a coyote can be seen on the clothesline. a howling sound soon follows. a scared alex witnesses this and hides behind the altar. an amused califas exits.)

alex. grandma?

(no response; beat. alex relaxes. he notices a toy plane on the altar. he picks it up and begins playing with it. after a few moments, marta enters, holding a white plastic shopping bag. she remains silent as she watches alex play. at one point, alex crashes the plane. it is obvious

by the expression on marta's face that this is a source of concern for her.)

marta. hola, alejandro.

(a startled alex stops playing with the plane.)

alex. where were you?
marta. i was across the street at connie's house, mijo. i needed to borrow some things.
alex. i didn't see anybody…and—
marta. i know, mijo…i know.

(extended beat. alex attempts to give his grandmother the toy plane.)

alex. here.
marta. you hold onto it, mijo… i'll let you find a spot for it on la ofrenda.
alex. you sure?

(marta nods her head. alex meticulously begins to walk around the altar. he wants to make sure he finds the perfect area to place the plane on. as he does, the shadow of a plane can be seen flying on the clothesline.)

marta. mijo…we build this ofrenda to honor those who have come before us. it must always be respected. sabes?
alex. …
marta. we honor our ancestors…our people.
alex. what do you mean our people?

marta. well…i mean our parents.

(alex stops; beat. he resumes walking.)

marta. our parents' parents. our grandparents' parents…a long line that traces back to the beginning…it's to celebrate the lives of those we've loved…and, even for those we didn't.

alex. that doesn't make any sense.

marta. it means we should never…not love anybody, mijo.

alex. oh.

marta. that is why our ofrenda is here, it's filled with bits and pieces of the past—pictures, favorite foods; just about anything. these things remind us that time stops for no one. entiendes?

alex. i think so.

marta. it's all right, mijo…rome wasn't built in a day… there's no rush.

alex. grandma?

marta. si?

alex *(staring at the toy plane)*. why do people hate each other so much?

marta. not everybody hates ea—

alex. but…some do.

marta. yes…i suppose they do. *(alex finally finds a spot for the plane; beat.)* why that spot, mijo?

alex *(looking at the ofrenda)*. it's on a runway…see, those skull things are surrounding it, making sure it's safe… and if you look at their eyes it looks like they're waiting for it to take off. *(beat.)* that's where it belongs.

marta. i think you're right, mijo. *(extended beat.)*

alex. this plane is more than just a toy, isn't it, grandma?

marta. si, mijo…we must honor the people who were on those planes that day…and, for the people who were in those buildings that day, as well. they need to know that they are still in our hearts.

alex *(somberly)*. can i go to my room, grandma?

marta. if you want, but i was hoping you could help me with just one more thing.

alex. okay, i guess.

(marta crosses to the plastic bag she had entered with. she walks to the front of the stage area, standing at the end of the marigold petal trail started from the back of the audience. a curious alex follows; beat.)

marta. close your eyes.

alex. what?

marta. close your eyes and reach into the bag.

alex. i don't know about this.

marta. aye, calmate…the bag won't bite.

alex. okay, okay. *(alex closes his eyes and reaches into the bag.)*

marta. don't pull out anything…enjoy it.

alex. enjoy what?

marta *(closing her eyes; pleased)*. shh…smell.

alex *(taking a sniff)*. it smells nice.

marta *(opening her eyes)*. reach out of the bag.

alex *(opening his eyes)*. they're flowers.

marta. they are the leaves of the cempasúchil.

alex. man…i'm not even going to try and say that.

marta. it's nahuatl for marigolds.

alex. what am i supposed to do with them?

marta. you and i are going to make a trail of them…all the way to the altar.
alex. why?

(at this point, a lit trail of marigolds can be seen on the clothesline; almost appearing like a string of bright orange-yellow christmas lights. we also see the silhouettes of the ancestors following the trail. marta grabs some petals. she begins dropping them as she slowly walks toward the ofrenda.)

marta. just do what i do. *(alex begins to follow marta's instructions.)* the spirits need all the help we can give them if they are to reach the ofrenda.
alex. why would ghosts nee—
marta. spirits, mijo, not ghosts…ghosts are for cartoons.
alex. what's the difference?
marta. ghosts are meant to scare. spirits are meant to protect.
alex. if they're protecting us, why are we helping them out?
marta. that's the funny thing, mijo…for some reason, the sweet smell of the petals guide the spirit of our ancestors to the ofrendas.
alex. that's sorta cool.
marta. i know…you know what else?
alex. what?
marta. they're blind, too.
alex *(amused)*. get out of here!
marta. de veras! *(gesturing.)* cross my heart.
alex. no way!
marta. the marigolds form a pathway for them.

alex. like the yellow-brick road?
marta. i never thought about it that way but, yes, in some sort of strange way.

(marta and alex reach the altar. they use the final marigold petals and spread them around the altar. once they complete this, the trail of marigolds and the ancestors fade away from the clothesline. alex and marta step back and admire their work; beat.)

marta. i think we did a pretty nice job. what do you think?
alex. i guess it looks all right.
marta. alex?
alex. yeah?
marta *(curiously)*. did you take the tamales off the altar?
alex. nope.
marta. are you sure? maybe, when you put the plane on?
alex. i swear, grandma…i didn't touch a thing.
marta. hmm…that's strange. ni modo. *(beat.)* me…you…us talking. this is nice? isn't it? *(marta puts her arm around alex. alex quickly pulls away.)* alex…mijo. what's wrong?
alex. nothing.
marta *(beat)*. i see so much of your mama in you. you know that?
alex. …
marta. you both share the same smile. *(beat.)* you know, alex, it's all right if you want to talk to me about your mama—
alex. no.
marta. it's all right, mijo…that's what she would want us to do. don't you think?

alex. …
marta. your mama is always watching over you.
alex. i don't want to talk about her.
marta. pero, alex…why not?
alex. i just don't, okay…it doesn't matter anyway.
marta. that's not true.
alex. it's not going to change anything.
marta. it will make her happy.
alex. then…you talk to her.
marta. she wants to talk to us.
alex. no.
marta. the ofrenda will make sure of it.
alex *(pointing)*. no, it won't…because if this thing was special, my mom and dad would've built one, too…but, they didn't believe in it and if they didn't, why should i!?
marta. alex!
alex. we don't need an altar and i don't want to talk to any spirits.
marta. you need to talk to your mama.
alex. stop acting like that!
marta. like what, alex?
alex *(angrily)*. like i only have a mom!
marta. que que?
alex. i heard you talking on the phone…about my dad.
marta. mijo…i didn't mean t—
alex. what did he ever do to you!?
marta. …
alex. you talk about how we should love each other, but you're not telling the truth! you didn't like my dad. i'm part of my dad so if you don't like him, you don't like me!

marta. that's not true, alejandro.
alex. alex! my name is alex!!!

(alex rushes into his bedroom; slamming the door. marta is stunned.)

marta *(to herself; ashamed)*. i'm sorry.

scene 12

(alex sits on his bed; looking down, his head between his legs. after a few moments, califas appears. he is enjoying the tamales that he had taken from the altar.)

califas *(mouth full)*. man…i love your abuela's tamales! i swear, vato. this is my favorite time of the year!
alex *(not looking up)*. those don't belong to you.
califas. they do now, carnalito.
alex. she thought i took them.
califas. then…you better tell granny it's not cool to perpetuate the negative stereotype of the male chicano man.
alex *(lifting his head)*. what…are you talking about?
califas. in a few years when you're leadin the grape protests, you'll understand. simon?
alex *(annoyed)*. whatever.
califas. hey…what's with the attitude? i thought we were becomin friends. you know, like chico and the man… loooooookin good!
alex. who?
califas. you're killin me, carnal…now i feel like an old man. do i look like a senior citizen to y—

alex. leave me alone. *(beat; somberly.)* am i going to die?
califas. way to change the subject little—
alex *(scared)*. am I? *(extended beat.)*
califas. yeah…you are. *(beat.)* one day.
alex. when?
califas. don't ask me.
alex. why?
califas. it's not in my job description.
alex. i want to know.
califas. so does everyone else.
alex. it scares me sometimes…thinking about dying. *(beat; overwhelmed.)* i don't want to die.
califas. simon. i can understand that.
alex. you can?
califas. it's a big deal, ese. it ain't no joke…goin from one world to the next.
alex. what about god?
califas. what about him?
alex. is there a heaven?
califas. it depends on how you look at it.
alex. what do you mean?
califas. what I'm sayin, carnalito, is that not all people see it the same way, sabes? different strokes for different folks. buddhists. catholics. muslums…take your pick.
alex. how do i know which way is the right way?
califas. it ain't a competition, ese.
alex. how do you see it?
califas. death is as much a part of life as life is a part of death.
alex. huh?
califas. one depends on the other.
alex. i still don't get i—

califas. don't be afraid.

alex. but, you said it was all right for me to be scared.

califas. bein scared and livin your life in fear are two entirely different things, little man...but, in time, you'll figure it out.

alex. how?

califas. how? why? what? where? who? chale, vato. trust me...okay? *(beat.)* this is the way it was meant to be.

alex *(defeated)*. but, what about—?

califas. stop chasin your tail, carnalito. *(extended beat. califas puts his hands together; forming a butterfly. he begins flapping his hands. he does this for a few moments. alex is mesmorized by this action. califas motions for alex to copy his hand gestures.)* they've been linked with the spirits of the dead. their images were carved in stone on many aztec monuments...flyin thousands of miles...millions of them...arrivin for dia de los muertos.

alex. who?

califas. the mariposas. the coolest. the baddest. the most firme butterflies of them all...the monarchs. *(beat.)* they're comin.

alex. here?

califas. of course...they're invited guests. *(beat.)* check it, little man...the day of the dead is about invitin the past.

alex. why?

califas. because you can't know where you're goin if you don't know where you've been...sabes?

alex. what does that mean?

califas. it means we all have stories, vato.

alex *(looking at his hands)*. nothing's happening.

califas. i wouldn't be so sure of that.

(the silhouette of a butterfly flapping its wings is projected on the clothesline. alex notices.)

alex. cool!
califas. simon…it's a beautiful sight, ese. *(beat.)* the picture in front of us…the myth.
alex. myth?
califas. the thin line between fact and fiction.

(more butterfly silhouettes can be seen on the clothesline.)

alex. more butterflies!
califas. all the way from mictlan…the land of the dead.

(a flurry of butterfly silhouettes flapping their wings can be seen on the clothesline. califas stops moving his hands. alex notices; beat. he stops as well.)

alex. check it out!
califas. the monarchs bear the spirits of the departed.
alex. departed?
califas. the dead.
alex. my…
califas *(beat)*. simon.
alex. i don't want them to be dead.
califas. they're not…not exactly.
alex. what does that mean?
califas. there are three deaths…los tres muertos.
alex. three?
califas. the first death is when our bodies no longer function. when our hearts no longer beat. when our gaze no

longer has depth…when the space we occupy slowly loses its meaning.

(some of the butterfly silhouettes disappear.)

alex. the second?

califas. it comes when the body is lowered into the ground and returned to la tierra. to mother earth…out of our sight.

(more butterflies disappear leaving only the silhouette of a lone butterfly flapping its wings.)

alex *(beat)*. and…the third one?

califas. the third death. the one that truly matters…is when there is no one left alive to remember us. *(califas raises his palm, face up and blows away the final butterfly from the projection; to alex.)* if you don't want to remember them…then, your parents truly are dead.

alex. they might not—

califas. not again, vato.

alex. my parents were nice people!

califas. simon. yes…and, those two nice people were inside those two buildings when they fell.

alex. why?

califas. i hate to break it to you, carnalito, but what happened on that day was a tragedy and tragedies happen all the time.

alex. why…them?

califas. why not? *(extended beat.)*

alex *(angrily)*. why couldn't those guys take someone else!? someone bad!

califas. it's not my place to say, carnalito.

alex. why do the bad people get to live for such a long time!?

califas. even i don't have the answer to that one. *(extended beat. califas slowly walks to the window and opens it. he begins exiting and stops; half of his body is outside, half is inside.)* adios, carna—

alex *(quietly)*. my parents...are good people.

califas *(shaking his head; frustrated)*. whatever you say, little alex.

scene 13

(marta is staring at the scribbling on the wall in alex's room; lost in thought. califas is standing behind her. after a few moments, califas walks over to the bed. he opens alex's lunchbox; beat. califas snaps his fingers. marta hears it and looks around the room, but she can't see califas. she does, however, notice that alex's lunchbox is open; beat. she decides to see what is inside. she notices the baseball cards and baseball. she also finds a picture of alex with his parents at a yankees game. she is about to cry, but she manages to keep her composure; extended beat. she closes the lunchbox and keeps the picture. marta and califas exit alex's bedroom and cross toward the ofrenda. she decides that she will place the picture on a prominent location on the altar. she does so and then she kneels in front of the ofrenda and begins praying; beat. the living room door opens; alex enters. he begins crossing to his bedroom.)

marta *(hurt)*. not even a "hi" grandma.

(alex stops, but doesn't bother to turn around.)

alex *(sulking)*. hi.
marta. what do you think, mijo!?
alex *(turning around)*. about what?
marta. your picture on the altar.
alex *(shocked)*. what!?
marta. the one with you and your mama y papa.
alex. no…how could you!? *(alex runs to the altar and "rips" his photo off the altar.)*
alex. how did you get this!?
marta. mijo, calmate.
alex. it was in my lunchbox!
marta. it was open, mijo…i just thought you would like your pic—
alex. don't you ever touch it again! this is my picture…not yours!
marta. si, mijo…lo siento.
alex. i don't want it on your altar…ever!
marta. alejandr—
alex. i never asked to come here! i want to go home!
marta. mijo, this is your home.
alex. no! don't say that!
marta. por favor, mi nieto…no te—
alex. why did my parents have to leave me!?
marta. alex, they did not leave you.
alex. yes, they did!
marta. they loved you.
alex. if it wasn't for them, i wouldn't be here!
marta *(pleading)*. it wasn't their fault, mijo!

alex. they left me all alone.
marta. pero, mijo…you are not alone.
alex. yes, i am.
marta. you have me.
alex. no, i don't. don't lie to me!
marta. alex…que dices!?
alex. you're going to leave me, too…just like everybody else!
marta. alex, i'm never going anywhere.
alex. you can't say that! you can't make that promise! everybody dies!
marta. mijo—
alex. i hate this place!
marta. alex, please!

(califas snaps his fingers. alex and marta freeze.)

califas. do what you gotta do, ese. *(califas snaps his fingers. alex and marta unfreeze.)*
alex. i wish i was never born!!!

(alex rushes to the the ofrenda and begins to throw items to the floor. a stunned marta begins to cry. as alex continues to destroy the ofrenda, marta kneels on the floor picking up a picture. alex finally stops fighting with the ofrenda and himself. he notices his grandmother on the floor crying, clutching a picture of her deceased husband.)

marta *(to herself)*. aye, mi esposo querido…my carlos.

(alex is stunned by this sight; not knowing what to do or what to say; extended beat. califas helps her up.)

alex *(apologetic)*. grandma…i'm— *(to califas.)* califas?
califas *(solemnly)*. don't look at me, ese…this is an a and b conversation…i'm c-ing my way out of it.

(califas kisses marta on the forehead and disappears. alex crosses toward marta, but he stops. he is not quite sure what to do; extended beat. alex rushes off into his room with marta still clutching the picture of her deceased husband.)

scene 14

(alex is sitting on his bed. marta is next to her destroyed ofrenda. they are both praying. an old picture of marta holding alex as a newborn is projected on the clothesline. note: the dialogue in this scene is staggered; one on top of the other.)

alex. god—
marta. —dios santo—
alex. —are you listening—
marta. —i need your guidance—
alex. —what's going to happen to us—
marta. —now more than anytime—
alex. —if things get worse—
marta. —turns his back—
alex. —stops loving me—
marta. —what to do, what to say—

alex. —i don't want her to think—
marta. —mi alejandro—
alex. —i don't love her—
marta. —mi vida. my life—
alex. —because i do—
marta. —my link to mija—
alex. —she's all i got—
marta. —lo quiero. i love him with all my heart—
alex. —and, dad—
marta. —jason—
alex. —i promise you i—
marta. —please forgive me. i—
alex. —am never ever ever—
marta. —going to—
alex. —forget you—
marta. —blame you—
alex. —you and me, dad—
marta. —put you—
alex. —yankees forever—
marta. —in the middle of everything—
alex. —but, i keep having the same bad dream—
marta. —what happened to our familia that morning—
alex. —i keep thinking that—
marta. —it was just our imaginations—
alex. —that you and mom are—
marta. —fooling us and that you two are—
alex. —going to walk through the door—
marta. —hiding the pain—
alex. —and that we would be—
marta. —living together as—
alex. —one big happy family again—
marta. —una familia unida—

alex. —like we used to be—
marta. —a family united as one—
alex. —mommy—
marta. —estrella— *(extended beat.)*
alex & marta. i miss you.

(scene fades to black.)

scene 15

(alex is sleeping. he is clutching his yankees lunchbox. califas is writing on the "scribble" wall. the low hum of traffic can be heard in the background. after a few moments, it is apparent that alex is in the midst of a nightmare. he wakes up in a cold sweat; beat. he composes himself a bit; noticing califas at the same time.)

alex. what are you doing?
califas. …
alex. i don't blame you. i wouldn't talk to me either.
califas. why is that, little man?
alex. you know why.
califas. simon.
alex. i'm sorry.
califas. you're talkin to the wrong person, homey.
alex *(beat)*. maybe…i'm the bad person.
califas. chale, little vato…no need to go drama queen. you're only human, sabes?
alex. …
califas. you're a chavalito…just a kid.

alex. still. *(extended beat. alex gets up from the bed and crosses to califas. he stands by him.)* you're taking up the entire wall.

califas. not much…considerin the size of the project.

alex *(begins to read off a few names)*. judith jones. michael ivory. scott powell. kip taylor…el, el, elk—

califas. elkin yuen.

alex. oh. *(beat.)* califas…what is this?

califas. a list.

alex. what kind of list?

califas. a list that lists names.

alex. there must be a couple of hundr—

califas. a couple of thousand…names.

alex. who are they?

califas. they're players in the box score of life, my man.

alex. i don't get it.

califas. just names, ese…nothing special.

alex. why bother?

califas. my thoughts exactly. *(califas turns toward alex and hands him the pen.)*

alex. what do you want me to do with this?

califas. complete the list.

alex. but…it looks finished.

califas. looks can be deceiving, que no?

alex. why me?

califas. because it's about your heritage…your warrior aztec blood…the blood runnin through your veins…through the veins of your abuelita. the blood you share.

alex. you're not making any sense.

califas *(sternly)*. it's your responsibility…your time to start livin the rest of your life, carnalito. *(beat.)* but, you can't do that until you finish the list.

alex. i still don't get—

califas. the list! it's missin two names and your parents aren't around to sign on the dotted line, homey.

(alex ponders these words; beat. he walks up to the wall and begins to run his hand down the wall; touching it gently.)

alex *(defeated)*. i can't, califas.

califas. sorry to hear that, vato.

(alex attempts to hand califas the pen back, but califas does not accept.)

alex *(quietly pleading)*. please…don't make me do it.

califas. if you don't want to sign it…fine. who am i to say anything. i don't care either way.

alex *(angrily)*. but…i do! *(extended beat.)*

califas. then, prove it, little man.

(extended beat. alex slowly inches up to the wall. he takes a deep breath and slowly begins writing. a picture of the wall is projected on the clothesline.)

alex *(to himself; subdued)*. jason erik smith. *(beat.)* estrella torres-smith. *(the projection of the list fades away.)*

califas. your parents were proud of you…i'm proud of you, ese.

alex. when will it stop hurting?

califas. it never will…but, it gets better.

alex. better?

califas. yeah.

alex. how soon?
califas. ain't no timeline for something like that.
alex. i wish it would stop hurting right now.
califas. simon, ese. lo siento, but life unfolds in its own way…you'll know when you know.
alex. know what?
califas. the answers to your questions.
alex. which questions?
califas. the ones—
alex *(solemnly)*. that matter.
califas *(beat; proudly)*. simon, carnalito…i think you're startin to get the hang of it.

(califas starts to exit. he crosses to the window. alex crosses to him and then stops; extended beat. alex stands there not saying a word, but knowing he doesn't have to.)

califas *(tenderly)*. you're the man of the house now. take care of your abuelita. entiendes, mendez?

(alex nods; beat. califas extends out his hand. califas slowly and respectfully shows alex the chicano handshake, then disappears.)

scene 16

(marta is sweeping up the living room. the virgen de guadalupe is projected on the clothesline. after a few moments, alex enters cautiously.)

alex. grandma?
marta. ...
alex. abuelita?

(marta is surprised by alex. she turns around and smiles at him; extended beat.)

marta. you wouldn't mind helping an old lady...would you?

(alex nods his head; beat. he crosses next to marta. they both discard items into a plastic bag for a few moments without saying one word to each other.)

alex. i'm sorry.

(extended beat. the image of the virgen fades away.)

marta. alex...grown-ups sometimes have trouble talk— *(beat; apologetic.)* about your papa. it was just that— *(marta crosses to another area of the living room to pick up something; partly out of guilt.)*
alex *(cautiously)*. you can call me alejandro... i mean, could you call me alex once in a while? i kinda like that name, too.
marta. okay, mijo...i'll do that.
alex. grandma?
marta. yes?
alex. what are we going to do?
marta. i'm not sure.
alex. i'm confused.

marta. that's all right, alejandro. at least, we'll be confused together…que no? *(alex nods his head; extended beat.)* today is the second day of november.

alex. day of the dead.

marta *(beat)*. we must rebuild this ofrenda…make it even better.

alex. okay.

marta. thank you for reminding me, mijo.

alex. about what, grandma?

marta. that sometimes i need to talk, too.

alex. grandma?

marta. que, mi angelito?

alex. i remember.

marta. que, mi angelito?

alex. i remember one thing about when i was really young…your hugs. how warm they were…they're just like mom's hugs.

marta. you mean that, mijo?

alex *(nods his head; beat)*. what next, grandma?

marta. we survive, mijo…can't ask for anything more.

alex. grandma…what if i forget?

marta. no, mijo…impossible. your parents are part of you forever. they are your protectors now…your angels. *(extended beat.)*

alex. mom and dad are safe now…aren't they?

marta. si, mijo…they are at peace.

(marta opens her arms. alex dives into them. it is the first time alex has allowed marta to touch him. marta embraces her grandson as the stage goes dark except for a lone spotlight which is focused on alex and marta; extended beat.)

alex. grandma?
marta. yes?
alex *(on the verge of tears)*. i can still miss my mom and dad…right?
marta *(tenderly)*. always, mijo.

(alex, in his grandmother's embrace, begins to sob loudly. it is the first time he has cried for his parents. marta is trying to keep her composure but, after a few moments, she begins sobbing alongside her grandson. lights fade to black and in the darkness, their crying can be heard as it slowly fades into silence.)

end of play

DIRECTOR'S NOTES